Barnard New Women Poets Series   Edited by Claudia Rankine

THE CHARACTER

Jena Osman

Introduction by Lyn Hejinian

For Julia —
Very nice meeting you!
all best,
Jena

Beacon Press   Boston

Beacon Press
25 Beacon Street
Boston, Massachusetts 02108-2892
www.beacon.org
Beacon Press books
are published under the auspices of
the Unitarian Universalist Association of
Congregations.

Printed in the United States of America
05 04 03 02 01 00 99   8 7 6 5 4 3 2 1
Portions of this work have appeared in the
following publications: *Abacus:* "Ellerby's
Observatory"; *Avec:* "Invention," "The Agrarian,"
"Hydra Village," "The Parrot: Distinction of
Awkward Shape, Allure of Deep Color";
Big Allis: "Odradek in Venice (2)," "Nineteen-
Thirties"; *Chain:* "Authorities (A Lecture)";
Combo: "Lag (I lag) Series; *Conjunctions:*
"The Character"; *O-blēk:* "Upbringing";
Re*Map: "The Drivers"; *Subliminal Time (O/4):*
"Odradek in Venice (1)," "Lepsy," "Dead Text,"
"Upbringing," "Industry of Balloons";
Tyuonyi: "Dialogue on the Locative Case";
Writing from the New Coast: "The Figural Cabinet"
(formerly titled "Ambiguities of Hyaline").

The Emily Dickinson poem on page 106 is
from fascicle 31, printed in *The Manuscript Books
of Emily Dickinson*, ed. R.W. Franklin, Harvard
University Press, 1981.

The April 1998 Supreme Court transcripts
extracted in the "found poem" in "Authorities
(A Lecture)" were culled from the Internet.
*This book is printed on recycled acid-free paper that
contains at least 20 percent postconsumer waste and
meets the uncoated paper ANSI/NISO specifications
for permanence as revised in 1992.*
TEXT DESIGN BY JULIA SEDYKH DESIGN
Library of Congress Cataloging-in-Publication Data
Osman, Jena
The character/Jena Osman; introduction by
Lyn Hejinian.
p. cm. —(Barnard new women poets series)
ISBN 0-8070-6847-0 (pbk.)
I. Title. II. Series.
PS3565.S6C47 1999
811'.54—dc21   98-48252

To My Parents

{ *Even if empathy, or self-identification with the character, can be usefully indulged in at rehearsals (something to be avoided in a performance) it has to be treated just as one of a number of methods of observation. . . . it is the crudest form of empathy when the actor simply asks: what should I be like if this or that were to happen to me? what would it look like if I were to say this and do that?— instead of asking: have I ever heard somebody saying this and doing that? in order to piece together all sorts of elements with which to construct a new character such as would allow the story to take place—and a good deal else. The coherence of the character is in fact shown by the way in which its individual qualities contradict one another.* }

—BERTOLT BRECHT,
"A Short Organum for the Theatre"

{ *I said that I knew very well what disorder consciousness causes . . .* }

—HEINRICH VON KLEIST,
"On the Marionette Theatre"

Contents

Introduction

The Character is new. Bold and intelligent and engaged in the irreverent task of perpetual self-invention, *The Character* is Jena Osman's first major publication, her work having until now appeared only in relatively transitory sites—as contributions to poetry magazines or in chapbooks. That work has been remarkable and remarked upon, however; magazines and chapbooks may be transitory but they are not without relevance and effect. And furthermore through her work as an editor (in particular of the influential magazine, *Chain,* which she co-edits with Juliana Spahr), Jena Osman has participated significantly in the emergence of a new generation of writers and in the formation of a poetics pertinent to that new body of work and its context.

The period in which we find ourselves now and in and of which Jena Osman writes is a post-postmodern one (although, happily, neither that label nor, to the best of my knowledge, any other has been applied to it). Ethical density, political ambiguity, shifting subjectivity, multifold social terrains, multicultural identities and interrelations— these are givens rather than discoveries in Jena Osman's work, and as a result the work doesn't stop with them. These constitute the setting in — which *the character* of these times finds itself.

Osman's interest in performativity is evident immediately and throughout this book, and something (though not everything) of her approach to it can be deduced from the two epigraphs which open the text. The first, from Bertolt Brecht, reminds us that character itself is performed, and that it represents not a reduction of complexity into an essential or representative type, into typicality, but rather that it is constituted through atypicality, nonidentity. The character is of many parts; or to put it another way, being of many parts is the part it plays.

Performance requires the person who is the actor (i.e., already a character) to be in character, and this, in turn, cannot occur without performance. This produces not a tautology ("performance requires performance") but a bifurcation—character occurring as a performance both in and of itself; or, as Osman says (in "The Figural Cabinet"), "the taking place is double."

Such double-mindedness, which is to say, this 'self'-consciousness, is central to Brechtian theater; it forms the basis on which alterities can come into (the) play. It is characteristic, too, of everyone who is forced into identity-consciousness, as W. E. B. Du Bois pointed out long ago in *The Souls of Black Folk*, a work which itself has been described (by Houston Baker) as a "cultural performance." More recently, the notion that "identity" is itself performative has been greatly elaborated by theorists such as Judith Butler. Identity—the sense of difference that belongs to one's self-sameness—is itself "character," something that "takes place." This means both that it is an occurrence or event— it happens—and that it involves taking up a position among others (as might be indicated by stage directions: *Enter Woman, wearing a hat,* etc.).

The second epigraph to the book is from Heinrich Von Kleist's "On the Marionette Theatre," and the various references to puppets in Osman's book add to the critical strangeness of the revolving character of the character. This is explicit in the title poem, which is also the first poem in the book, a tour de force which embodies its own performance, carrying on at various levels, and most obviously through intertextual devices (quotations from and/or allusions to other texts) and through footnoted footnotes, a dialogue in and of itself. One of these footnoted footnotes quotes and comments on a passage from Meyerhold (see page 4). An exegesis of it produces a sequence of replacements: real people are replaced by (become) actors, actors are

replaced by puppets, puppets are replaced by characters, the characters
become increasingly real. The becoming that is involved here is enacted
through a sequence of removes, "so that the first character / may be
captured by the second." This reproduces "reality 'as it really is'":
"the body of the first has many more parts / whereas it is possible to
make out / the complexion, the dreams, of the second" ("The Figural
Cabinet").

Our awareness of the separate moving "parts" of a puppet
alerts us to its status as a *what;* it is a who becoming a what. But, at the
same time, because the puppet is a character, it is also true the puppet
is a what becoming a who. The character in puppet form is familiar but
alien, human but inhuman, *heimlich* but *unheimlich.*

The degree to which the workings of language can be similarly
described is important for an understanding of this book. That the
materials of language, its letters, are sometimes called "characters"
is more than coincidental. And the fact that the limited repertoire of
such characters can form (or perform) an infinite array of meaningful
configurations (words and, more importantly, sentences), contributes
to the sense of originality and vitality that characterizes the works.

In and through its performances, the character in each of its
forms is always in a state of invention and a condition of becoming.
It is always, therefore, acting in a state of temporality; time is its
circumstance. Without time, the character couldn't act, couldn't react,
couldn't perform—or to put it another way, time is that through
which character forms. And because of this, as it takes place, it takes *baloney!*
on features, of itself and of its world.

And this is where, through the prevalent use of theatrical devices,
Osman admits an ethical element to her work. The dialogic techniques
(including both intertexual and intratextual layerings), in allowing
the work to question itself, require it to be answerable to itself. The
particular quality of double-mindedness that this produces functions as
one of the work's various "alienating" or "distancing" devices,

enhancing the effect of the footnoting in "The Character"; the metacommentaries that occur in, for example, sections of "Ellerby's Observatory"; the incongruencies and hilarious absurdities in the verbatim 'real life' performance of the Supreme Court justices in "A Real Life Drama" that's appended to "Authorities: A Lecture"; the interruptions that occur in and to the text in the form of stage directions, ellipses, abutted discourses ("our host greeting us at the door. / (although you can never be sure)" ["Ellerby's Observatory"]); the intruding voices, authorial or faux authorial (author as character) commentary, etc.; and the merging of criticism and creativity ("questions opacity / questions transparency" ["Invention"]) that occurs throughout the book. These provide what Osman at one point (in "Invention") calls "separation": "The characters," she points out, "depend on separation in order to function together and form an ethical completeness."

This separation creates a location that can be termed interest: *inter est*—it is between. That which is of interest, that which is between, is what allows for the exuberant inventiveness of the poetry and it is there that our interest in it, our enthusiasm and caring, develop. The character of interest is not a type but an ethicality. Hence Osman's concern for the question—the weighing—of "justice," which is forcefully presented in "Authorities (A Lecture)." There she implies a relationship between literary lineation and legalistic delineation as she plays off the homonymic relation of *sentence* in the linguistic sense to *sentence* in the judicial sense.

To posit *character* as an ethical dimension is, of course, something that ordinary usage of the word allows; we use the term to refer to the degree and power of someone's moral virtue (or lack thereof). And just as the performance of personality requires action, so too does the performance of ethics, with the result that examination of character in this sense must involve a consideration of power—the will to power and the expression of it, the different forms power might take, the ideas, things, or qualities in relation to which one might have power, and the uses to which it is put.

Historically, and until very recent times, women have generally been made to feel that any evident personal interest in power on their part would be an embarrassment. They have been discouraged even from addressing the question of power, being expected either to concede it (to men), or to disguise or reject it, or simply to consider it of no relevance or interest to them. To covet power was thought to be unfeminine, and to exercise it was regarded as monstrous. And, with some very important exceptions (in the work of Carla Harryman, Bernadette Mayer, and Susan Howe, for example), even in recent times the issue has remained in the background of writing by women.

Jena Osman's work, however, does take on the question of power and in particular that modality of power that is inherent to invention. The creative power of invention is manifest throughout this book. It invests the writing with liveliness, with *energeia*—*act*uality—and with it the capacity for activating thought; and, since every action is also a beginning, generating effects and therefore more action, the writing performs its own (perpetually changing) creative character.

The investigatory power of invention is both structural and thematic in this book. An investigatory method is implicit in the numerous and various dialogic structures of the poems and in the self-reflexive gestures that often occur in the text. And it is the explicit in some of them—as, for example, in "from The Periodic Table as Assembled by Dr. Zhivago, Oculist" and in the three sections ("liquid air," "X, or Roëntgen Rays," and "wireless telegraphy") of the poem entitled "Invention."

But the power to invent does not (and cannot) provide one with the power to control. Invention always involves unpredictability and incompleteness; intrinsic to it is the possibility of infinitude. And not only does invention initiate events which it can't control; the inventor, in the end, is herself a character—she too is invented.

Her subjectivity exists and has autonomous reality, but primarily in the sense that it is subject *to* things. It consists of intersubjectivity; it exists in connections. Subjectivity is on strings, amid lines. Precisely for this reason, it is human; "The line is that which 'humanizes' imagination," Osman writes ("Authorities: A Lecture"). And it is, in the end, the human who is *the character* of the title and the hero of this wonderful new book.

—LYN HEJINIAN

The Character

The Character

It was a fair trial. The body proves the process and the animal shows its wool. This is an idea that allows for immediate access. The fair was not a trial, but a place to show the animals. The man was an animal, and thus his trial was fair.[1] This is not an aesthetic sphere. The equation shifts as analogical contexts reach out and shake the snowflakes over the dome of the city.

see a world salute a sir
who sets a table
and sues the national object
and kills and keels and
bloodies the tent
the hand that pours judicial seizure[2]

detachment, there's order; order is the fruit of action[3]

---

[1]. Can we really fault the Russian director Meyerhold for not mentioning the Russian fairground, but instead placing all of his attention on French and Italian models?[a]

[2]. The proceedings were complex and required intense concentration; however, N.L. and I found our attention wandering to the man who filled the water pitchers that were placed before the justices. He wore lime green slacks.

[3]. Action or animation? It is possible to perceive animation in a completely inactive subject— even in a subject that is dead.[b] There is no perception without attachment.

---

[a]. can we fault you for delimiting the justice system within an aesthetic sphere?

[b]. "Attachment is a manufacturer of illusions and whoever wants reality ought to be detached." —SIMONE WEIL

this suspect sets a table of fatality[4]

Innocence applies to the character in the way that fine china applies to a whale. At least in the eyes of the many rides that trauma the body on its way up and down. Amusements: perhaps you've seen him?[5] The lines in his hands coincide with the lines on which you wait hour after hour, at the end of which you cash in your ticket and fall up and into the sky. The gavel always strikes him, it strikes him now and again.[6]

a jeer
over part of necessity
I
pull past the fair outerly
past an action.
might a sort of passivity
agitate action?[7]

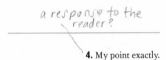

a response to the reader?

---

4. My point exactly.

5. Meyerhold writes: "In [the director's] attempts to reproduce reality 'as it really is,' he improves the puppets further and further[c] until finally he arrives at a far simpler solution to the problem: replace the puppets with real men."[d]

6. See Bill Irwin's "The Courtroom."

7. "We want receiving centers for dots and dashes." —H.D.

---

c. in other words, the actors

d. in other words, the character

Bill Irwin: actor, clown, writer

"a rest, sit close a while *— Emma Lazarus-esque*
the sick, the contrary
the following that I speak of
a rest, they'll have a rest"[8]

You purchase a future. It has nothing to do with bars or weights or balance. Look at your punishment as a purchase.[9]

the author of himself's complication

so that one plus one and he   *one — stabbing*
one plus one and he[10]

effort to withhold
a so-called someone in the hold of the boat
the sail as contract
sinking environment[11]

the guard did order
superior orders, infinitely under
put over the other sea sea green
grainy, etc.
contact the circle tangent to discretion
let them know we are here
to enter society

---

8. For indeed they must rest. The costumes she had designed for them treated the body
as an axis from which their limbs could only pivot.

9. Emerson wrote: "The least change in our point of view gives the whole world a pictorial air.
A man who seldom rides, needs only to get into a coach
and traverse his own town, to turn the street into a puppet-show."

10. "Do not presume too much upon my love; I may do that I shall be sorry for."[e]

11. "A ship is a habitat before being a means of transport . . . the enjoyment of being enclosed
reaches its paroxysm when, from the bosom of this unbroken inwardness,
it is possible to watch, through a large window-pane, the outside vagueness of the waters, and
thus define, in a single act, the inside by means of its opposite." — ROLAND BARTHES[f]

---

e. in other words, Cassius *— Caesar*

f. see "Cabins" by Max Beckmann
painting

"Knock, knock; never at quiet!
What are you?" **12**

the good me, more
a part pieced across the storm
I
leave a mark
on the destructed
hillock bound

I swear it
I crossed over and then
I fell in

"do you play what the others play
at the beach
by the water
in the core?" **13**

---

12. I've seen this porter portrayed as a vaudevillian. "Anon, anon! I pray you,
remember the porter." **g** Laughter is the societal urge, yet laughter
is also that which is most aberrant.

13. The character said this in his sleep. **h**

---

g. in other words, Macbeth

h. or was it you?

The essay is not another thing:
the mis-knowing of the man
is there
The guilty, even his story
is proof of experiments
of conscience[14]

that power is something,
she thinks

whereby a reader is pushed from the page[15]

continuous assault
of fuss

---

14. Or of annotation.

15. {Turn page over a couple of times very exaggeratedly}[i]

experience _____

i. {turn page over a couple of times very exaggeratedly}

poor attendant detached from
that to be attended, misfortune,
misfortune suffices not
he fights consolation, the
attendant[16]

there we meet our friend[17]

good resides in us inasmuch
as good exists in anything
the hourly thought I thank you sir
and sit down father
rest you—[18]

---

16. Is that related?[j] I have to agree with you there.[k] I'm not sure.

17. In other words, the character.

18. I would like to talk—

---

j. it seemed a bit frivolous to me

k. why don't we chat like this more often?

across destruction it is light
not the consolation—love—
it is light
a self transported from letters
into things, the letters themselves
sir, speed you;
what's your will?—[19]

attachment succeeds in an interior
however, illusory;
in this place resides a city
and within resides the border skeleton
our eye skids the steel wall of it[20]

"Then there's life in't."

there's meaning in being king
—King Lear

"Sa, sa, sa, sa."[21]

runs away mad

---

[19]. I actually have something I'd like to say—

[20]. But I've lost my notes.[l]

[21]. King Lear comes back to the surface, and admits that he knows Gloucester.[m]

---

[l]. don't you recognize me? can't you see me? your voice sounds so familiar . . .

[m]. but will he acknowledge me?

ELLERBY'S OBSERVATORY

for Antonio Sindorf

Loss of words or their repetitions.
An eternal problem here in a tropical ore.
Forest or is that forest of rain.
Avoiding certain passages.
Handing out the papers not quite.
The original idea of a decent life.
Each time such loss has countered.
A fair amount of play into the state.
Distraught even if the absent ones.
A better brand of music.
Equation not so simple.

You can easily translate the Spanish one somehow. Somehow the Spanish one, take his hand while in the car. While in the car his eyes practically rolling up towards the top of his head. Towards the top of his head and leaning against the wall. Against the wall of the sink this proving to be of interest. Of interest although blue. Blue but necessary for story line. For theatricality. You say nice night. So it is.

staged:	seams up the back of the legs
accompaniment:	an accordion she plays are you Jacques Brel
	not knowing him and her harmonica
appreciation:	backtalk
locale:	along the side wall
	churchbells
appreciation:	fingers on that other side wall

observation of flatness as his head touches his arm as he leans close to the arm resting on the tabletop in front of the window a window seat the mouth moving as if to eat but not quite succeeding because of the snow tilted to the ground and cold which determines hands and their ability to grasp keys and letters and the forgetfulness inherent to this position dominated by a head grazing an arm and the discussion of flatness.

It was a small brownstone with wooden shutters,
	(such is a memory procedure we think)
window plants and panes cut in the shape of diamonds;
	(as if within precautions or speed limits)
the kind of home that would make the most steadfast wanderer
	(the set noise of these tappings and the flowers)
want to take off his shoes and settle in. We entered
	(trees crashing against the glass or pressing out)
and immediately I felt myself give in to the comforting
	(and answering to circumstance such a reaction)
guessing game of what might lie in store for us
	(causing interest amongst several admirers all anonymous)
as guests of this house.
	(trees crashing against the glass or pressing out)
This was Ellerby's house, a part of him unknown to me.
	(or connected to personal history which might be interesting)
We arrived on the early side, our host greeting us at the door.
	(although you can never be sure)
He seemed in high spirits and listed for us the guests expected
	(wishbone fingers this sector not so interesting)
with great animation.
	(necessity of the domestic overwhelms certain moments
	and allows us to forget that this tune always carries
	us down the wrong aisle and up weak ladders . . .

What if the forest were to lose its repetitions.
How often would you sing good-night.
The star crops the gladiators the animals in the flower beds.
That forest a release of memory.
Pertaining to childhood yet artificial.

In Spain there is an indescribable red. Indescribable red which is not possibly imagined. Imagine your own lips and what is written on the labels. On the labels the recipe for his blue eyes. His blue eyes and her lips forming the word "el." The condemnation of all sorts of spice. All sorts of spice surely pertaining to the obvious discrepancy. Disjunction caused by the fact of youth. The fact of youth and its constant process towards Americanization.

accident: abandonment
accident: locked in its room without access
accident: what became of her fingers
accident: during times of crisis certain conveniences
               must be sacrificed
churchbells: night-pattern of shoes

observation of a rest as her hand touches the bindings her hand reads the
numbers while she continues to move down the rows of books not look-
ing at them although understanding their colors most of which are green
and the inevitable halting before a certain number as her hand registers
its presence or simple absence.

The dancing went on for hours. I glanced across the room
          (the reaction by this time causing interest)
to where I had left Ellerby just minutes before.
          (the ladders leading into the windows)
His lighthearted mood had at some point in the evening
          (within the domestic a circumstance which overwhelms)
worn thin.
          (is what music is made of we think)
"Yes," my partner replied; "I noticed that too!"
          (a mistake of the flowers not easily forgiven . . .

where is its
pair?

Now repetition considered usual.
The decent life manufactured or mined from ore.
What if a migration were to take place.
What if the restlessness in the downstairs kitchen.
The forest giving over to.
Tropical.
Singing smooth as a betrayal or face.

The plot remained vague although somewhat theatrical. Somewhat theatrical in his relating the day's events. The day's events not evident in what you say. What you say somehow abandoned within the car. Within the car a map of Spain. The theatricality of that which is foreign. That which is foreign a condemnation of story. Story providing the color blue and the appearance of character.

guideline:	not known Jacques
deux:	posthumes
fête:	par des chevaliers
le fils:	des étoiles
danses:	gothiques
pages:	mystiques
Satie:	seams up the back of the legs

The observation of his body as his movements prove substitutes for words although unsuccessful as his hands form a wall pushing quickly to the side what is being pushed pursued by the hands and the hips moving to the right as if about to break into a hit musical this perhaps at some other time charming and yet his arms so sadly different from those of the window.

I no longer sensed the presence of an underlying
        (the procedure consisting of walking or standing)
harmony.
        (requiring many details from the subject's life . . .

Equation how a dream is.
Pursued like a dog.
A stretcher lies between.
Equation of woods out back.
The stone wall what lies.
Beneath you guess stone.
What along the wall.
Equation along the wall.
Trespass with you?
What counters wire.
Loss and the guards.

The Spanish one with hands in the leaves. Hands in the leaves they swing legs to the wall. To the wall a sound springs lyrical. Lyrical being a word he always uses. He always uses the legs for the ash. The ash proving difficult in the thick of conversation. Her wish to remove what was just spoken. What was spoken retracted as they seek separate houses. His house containing a green pumpkin on a table.

accordion and harmonica:
war stories:
city divide of:
voice:

flows
coherence?

observation of the matches lit one by one let loose by skills on a ladder of
canvas lit soft so as not to wake but lost to breezes consistent somehow
disheartened.

I asked whether she would like a drink, wondering to myself
    ("there is an order to my childhood")
if such an evening might be salvageable after all.
    ("the name of my house a label or letter")
She weakly attempted a joke.
    ("let me carry you in and out of doors")
I laughed, but my mind of course was still on events
    ("under glass")
which remain unclear even to this day.
    ("I have caught you
     "I have won you . . .

Odradek in Venice (1)

{ *One is tempted to believe that the creature
once had some sort of intelligible shape and is
now only a broken-down remnant. Yet this
does not seem to be the case . . .* }

—FRANZ KAFKA,
"The Cares of a Family Man"

Accurate spinnings and a body offshooting, making good on the turn, brake, commute, be there up on one wheel. This is accurate because we can see it. Then again, no.

As with a kit he is put together, a mass of loose ends. A dose of persuasion and fury allows the charge to act as speed, and thus, disappearing. Be forever in his presence and you, too, might build a bridge.

No banks to either side.

At a certain point, you, too, may be recognized for what you once were. Then again, no. He lives in a finely painted house where a yard grows and a soldier stands. Light on the feet, over the wheel, up the road.

The speeches lapse the eye behind into a previously hidden corner or closet. That's how we see. And through this cloudy glass we can make out his mechanics. They reach to resound and yet pull back *before* sound.

Gloucester sees—"I know thee well enough"—but first an evidence in a flash of light. What he once was is outside like a frightened bolt. He reaches in to greet it, casts it deep into a pocket, whirs to the other side. To continue with speed and to act as lineage. This is how he sees.

ODRADEK IN VENICE (2)

traces in the ivory lead him out. he is the last part of a trail which you have followed. his path is due to the whims of your conception, a ribbon on a pole. with years, the gradients are tested, the steps that happen on the shifting plates—such movement only told, never felt—easily replicated by a diagram or gesture of a flattened hand. every inch of his manner indicates a stumbling transition; a desire for simpler planes.

having met you, his face appears more doll-like. is it the wind continually howling or your growing need to lie down flat in your own preoccupations? the sun itself refuses to reflect the everyday. instead, small steps click through the metropolis. this place, an oven to your foreignness, breeds a certain formality, he is swathed in those robes. he seems thinner, his expression changing according to the light.

why follow any further? you know everything he will tell you. certainty of his disappearance is what keeps you grilled to the activity. day in and out. the box had a special significance, but what it was is mostly lost. to hold an object representative of a regal idea. now the memory is lit by a small bulb in a much larger room.

the pole fits down his back and leads to a balance. he spins the perfect plate at the end of a stick. you notice, as he boards, that the legs have been incorrectly carved while the water vessel hides its purpose and he digs the ditch further. you feel if you encountered him in daily life you'd be quite sure of the next steps within the box. are the physical things in place? have they been marked by the eye and left there to sit? you wonder if his breath had been diabase (a city), would his disappearance be less clear.

takes place partly in, what do I mean "takes place"?
the top of it the same
if not always of glass

open the eyes in water
and see how matter is rearranged
under one color, within a single substance
only cold

where first I received an invitation
I left in order to breathe

now rise to the surface
on which books are laid

the tropics
of crystallite body

born in a gutter pipe
on a street of houses

the shape makes little sense
an object rolling by the stairs
or in a room near the children

never preceded by emotion;
however, resulting in that

which promotes the transparency
of emotion

a language of law

breath of rattling leaves
gust of the character
who pursues an activity

or stakes in the ground

the taking place is double
both in the green lawn and
observation tower,
water

under the water and also
by the side of that which calls
the stair a room, then roam

be near and touch the glass
that surrounds the skin
a coating mere the body falls in

released less plurally

and found like a light on top
swings across the dark moving

by suggestion drowned
the liquid foment and observation
hanged

walls, cantilevers, core wire, slag
our custom of looking inward
for the slightest burning

on the street

then the eye becomes an ornament
and the profile is only a vase
the body is simply a gesture
and the spine leaps into the neck

I know this building

the instruments have become part

and parcel of endless anatomy
and sound grows strange

so the night-watch opens its eyes

rain blackening the street
into a sweat of light voices,
glass hydrants,
spires

a glance, a sheath of lines
so that the first character
may be captured by the second
and then relax in a chair

the body of the first has many more parts
whereas it is possible to make out
the complexion, the dreams, of the second

no release from the construction I'm afraid—
questions will be taken later

one can only look more closely
imagine the sharing of radiants
piercing the heart of the beheld

part of the roof is in hand
against the chest of the figure
as a blank parallelogram
where ribs, organs, functions
should be—
not this fluorescent siding
that keeps us dry in the rain

others are the shape of banisters
through which
we see parts

is that a shield
or a huge drum hunching his back
upon the stairs which lead to a wall
above which perches a circular
drum

next, the bodies are dead
one hand is a peg
the helmet a star
the arching backs dead
in compliance with set

convertible architecture is necessary
in a sea of hyaline
much less across a portable sky
a configuration is when
the eye cannot see
thus scorns a wealth of knowledge
and a host of patrons

I cannot let myself go
down into the street

where the people have turned into hens
and the birds, in turn, are foxes

I say, but isn't this story
about a house, a neighborhood,
a small town before or after a war?

to be replied "relax"
under the spot, this streetlight:
now softshoe now windblow
now gesture now tophat

From THE PERIODIC TABLE
AS ASSEMBLED BY DR. ZHIVAGO, OCULIST

for my father

{ *I once heard a scientist who loves poetry say,*
the language of science and the language
of poetry have in common that they are both
natural languages under stress. }

—JOAN RETALLACK

1A 1																7A 17	0 18
1 **H** 1.008	2A 2											3A 13	4A 14	5A 15	6A 16	1 **H** 1.008	2 **He** 4.003
3 **Li** 6.941	4 **Be** 9.012											5 **B** 10.81	6 **C** 12.01	7 **N** 14.01	8 **O** 16.00	9 **F** 19.00	10 **Ne** 20.18
11 **Na** 22.99	12 **Mg** 24.31	3B 3	4B 4	5B 5	6B 6	7B 7	8	8B 9	10	1B 11	2B 12	13 **Al** 26.98	14 **Si** 28.09	15 **P** 30.97	16 **S** 32.07	17 **Cl** 35.45	18 **Ar** 39.95
19 **K** 39.10	20 **Ca** 40.08	21 **Sc** 44.96	22 **Ti** 47.88	23 **V** 50.94	24 **Cr** 52.00	25 **Mn** 54.94	26 **Fe** 55.85	27 **Co** 58.93	28 **Ni** 58.69	29 **Cu** 63.55	30 **Zn** 65.39	31 **Ga** 69.72	32 **Ge** 72.61	33 **As** 74.92	34 **Se** 78.96	35 **Br** 79.90	36 **Kr** 83.80
37 **Rb** 85.47	38 **Sr** 87.62	39 **Y** 88.91	40 **Zr** 91.22	41 **Nb** 92.91	42 **Mo** 95.94	43 **Tc** (99)	44 **Ru** 101.1	45 **Rh** 102.9	46 **Pd** 106.4	47 **Ag** 107.9	48 **Cd** 112.4	49 **In** 114.8	50 **Sn** 118.7	51 **Sb** 121.8	52 **Te** 127.6	53 **I** 126.9	54 **Xe** 131.3
55 **Cs** 132.9	56 **Ba** 137.3	57 *•La 138.9	72 **Hf** 178.5	73 **Ta** 180.9	74 **W** 183.9	75 **Re** 186.2	76 **Os** 190.2	77 **Ir** 192.2	78 **Pt** 195.1	79 **Au** 197.0	80 **Hg** 200.6	81 **Tl** 204.4	82 **Pb** 207.2	83 **Bi** 209.0	84 **Po** (209)	85 **At** (210)	86 **Rn** (222)
87 **Fr** (223)	88 **Ra** 226.0	89 †Ac 227.0	104 **Rf** (261)	105 **Ha** (262)	106 φ (263)	107 **Ns** (262)	108 **Hs** (265)	109 **Mt** (266)									

PERIODIC TABLE
OF THE ELEMENTS

	58 **Ce** 140.1	59 **Pr** 140.9	60 **Nd** 144.2	61 **Pm** (145)	62 **Sm** 150.4	63 **Eu** 152.0	64 **Gd** 157.3	65 **Tb** 158.9	66 **Dy** 162.5	67 **Ho** 164.9	68 **Er** 167.3	69 **Tm** 168.9	70 **Yb** 173.0	71 **Lu** 175.0
* Lanthanide series														
† Actinide series	90 **Th** 232.0	91 **Pa** 231.0	92 **U** 238.0	93 **Np** 237.0	94 **Pu** (244)	95 **Am** (243)	96 **Cm** (247)	97 **Bk** (247)	98 **Cf** (251)	99 **Es** (252)	100 **Fm** (257)	101 **Md** (258)	102 **No** (259)	103 **Lr** (262)

Note

This is a fragmentary hard-text rendition of what is meant to be a hypertext poem.
While reading this poem on a computer screen, clicking on bolded "elements"
leads the reader to small poems. Screens for small poems then direct the reader to put into
motion one of several "chemical reactions," which causes poems to be randomly
generated as words come into contact with each other through a computer program.
A rough hypertext version of this draft (posted in 1997) can be found at
the Electronic Poetry Center at *http://wings.buffalo.edu/epc/authors/osman.*

here are the elements that contribute to sight

Harness to Hydrogen
aeriform
the lightest body known
extinguishes burning bodies
dragoman, an interpreter
closely fitted in different languages
it signifies furniture and utensils
gig chaise casque sword buckler tackle
within which in its primary sense
it is synonymous as a horseman

IA

1 **H**arness
3 **Li**nks
11 **Na**rcotics
19 **K**ings
37 **R**obber **B**arons
55 **C**omputer **S**cientists
87 **Fr**enchmen

Links to Lithium
petalite has it
recovered from brines
a minor ingredient
in the telescope at Palomar
petalite passacaglia
dry cell stone

Narcotics to Sodium
the youth was his own headache remedy,
reflection of caustic salt:
—ike (—yke) —ick
swallow, inhale, inject the D lines of the sun and stars
this later Daffodil

Computer Scientists to Cesium
latin for two bright lines in the blue
attacks glass, reacts with ice
electrolysis of the fused cyanide sky

Frenchmen to Francium
It was 1939 and Mlle. Marguerite Perey of the Curie Institute incorrectly named the
ship after an ancient Gaul. Frencisce menn. Frensc mon. Frankis man. Frensshe men.
At any one time you can only find 17 atoms/people in the whole earth. How do we
know? A daughter has a half-life of 22 minutes. The leaves are tall and spirey and the
Virginians (incorrectly?) decided they were French.

there is a field that's protected by a screen
the screen sheds light
and bodies,
their shadows,
are available
but only partially

IIA

4 **Be**es
12 **Mi**lligrams
20 **Ca**sks of Armontillado
38 **S**eniors
56 **Ba**bies
88 **Ra**yguns

Milligrams to Magnesium
does not occur uncombined
with dolomite
combines
from brines
wells
incendiary sea water
and graphite cast

Casks of Amontillado to Calcium
burns yellow-red
a "getter"

Babies to Barium
heaviness is distinguished from lime by a doll,
a small image of the self reflected in someone else's
eye
keep it in a liquid that excludes air
the image decomposes in water
but can then be used for rat poison
foolish fellow

Rayguns for Radium
Madame Curie discovered us in the pitchblende
and no subject since has so interested the mind
of the general public. Next in line was the discovery
of a radius of light, generic weaponry for all.
Carmine red, sealed in minute tubes, the cartoon hero
shouts through the cancer he is forced to inhale.
We can be extracted and used to cure our own ills.

partial knowledge of a body
barely makes an element

IIIB

21	
Scientists	
39	
Youth	
57	
*****La**gs	
89	
+Acids	

Scientists to Scandium

violent metals inside conscience
Mendeleev predicted its existence
with a misnomer abundant in the sun and stars
under the stadium lights
cultivators of theoretic truths
give speeches about practical work
while artists sit in the bleachers
with the uranium mill tailings

Youth to Yttrium

at the beginning, lunar rock
resolved into the earths of three elements
unstable in air
then a quarry of color tv's
a village of europium phosphors and microwave filters
then scaly luster of simulated diamond studs
first a society of bell-ringers
then a generation of nuclear capture

*Lag (I lag) Series

{ *The northerly strip comprises a family of remark-*
ably similar metals known as the rare earths or,
more formally, the lanthanides . . . The lanthanides
are so similar to one another that until recently
they could be separated only with great difficulty.
Indeed, the near uniformity of their features
suggests that it is not really worth making the
considerable effort to separate them. Nature has
seemingly no use for the lanthanides in its contriving
of life, and humanity has only recently found
certain sporadic uses for these regions. }

—P.W. ATKINS,
The Periodic Kingdom

58	59	60	61	62	63	64	65	66	67	68	69	70	71
cell	pry	nod	pam	sum	euro	gad	tub	dye	hot	err	time	yob	luff

Ceres in prison
found on the beaches and river sands
as in a honeycomb
the inner level
and various organelles
small, humble abode
likely to ignite
if scratched with a knife

green twin inquisitor
isolated a new earth
a snoop
gave salts of different colors
a lever, a crow bar
a cigarette lighter
carbon arc in a welder's eye
pry a welder's eye

neo-twin agrees quickly
extracted from a rose
fractionation of sleep
sways, droops, flowers in the wind
lapse of light flint
to express and summon
silvery double

Prometheus stole fire
the jack of clubs and highest trump
workers at Ohio State confirmed it
abbreviated treatise
completely missing from the earth's crust
partisan writer
captures light in pale blue or greenish glow
little yet known

silvery luster stable in air
adding numbers in long half-lives
used to dope crystal, the central idea
the gist of lasers
excited in the infrared
condensed coercive forms
ignite in air

Europe is a deposit on the walls
identified in the sun and certain stars
countries of doped plastic and color tv
abducted to Crete in the form of a bull

fast burnout rate for son of Jacob
roams and roves as alpha form
this film which spalls off
with little purpose
like a spike in dry air
body-centered, close-packed
wandering garnets

the coal car left the mine
with grams of rare earth
in a tantalum crucible
dark as the moon
wider than it was deep
the masses lapped against the sides
"handle with care"
or the vessel will break
or the phosphor will fall

imparting color
hard to get at
readily attacked
dissolved
evolved
with hydrogen
calcium
color imparted
neutron bombardment

· hot Stockholm
burning chemists
announced the existence of "element X"
few uses for the acute toxic
fiery radioactive higher than normal
violent raging recently stolen
hot and bothered hot to trot
hot under the collar
hot making it hot for
unusual magnetic properties
only a few uses have been found for

in 1860, terbia was known as erbia
after 1877, erbia became terbia
the usage panel was split on the matter
56% preferred ûr
in the potassium vapor
violation of pronunciation
and ion-exchange
deflates the moral standard
isolated sin in enamel glaze

time was the earliest name for Scandinavia
was discovered in 1879
was the least abundant of the rare earth elements
only a few years ago, time was not obtainable
at any cost
time was silver-gray, soft, malleable
and could be cut with a knife
now a bomb, a capsule, a card
a clock and a deposit

hooligan, face-centered
keep it in a closed container
throw the word backwards
so the ruffian reacts slowly with water
electrical resistance increases tenfold
when it becomes a boy
a destructive youth spelled backwards

a catalyst in cracking
sailing closer into the wind
to steer Paris
closer into the wind
sails flapping
most costly
sails

am I losing my sight?
here is an element that occludes sight

Titles to Titanium

on the analogy of Uranium, named after his father
born on a meteorite called "oxide"
his prominence is renowned in the spectra of M-type stars
the ash of coal, the human body
expresses the worth of gold
which burns in air
Mr. So and So disperses higher than a diamond
converts sea water into fresh water
contends for legendary status
The crowd resists and gasps—
"I will now exhibit the asterism of a sapphire"—
in a permanent way
(no smoke screen)

Zeros to Zirconium

Persian nought
marking days with a cipher
worthless linear feet
heat ceases
functions vanish
the attack is timed to begin
"in the zero atmosphere of America" (Hawthorne)
rayon spinnerets
lamp filaments
heat shock

IVB

22 **Ti**tles
40 **Z**eros
72 **H**alf
104 **R**ifles/**Ku**ll

Half to Hafnium

The oldest sense in all languages is
"nuclear submarine." Heat a filament,
then gather oxygen. Mix with a sponge.
Call your agent. Get a petition going.
Lose all connexion with nautical discoveries.
Plead guilt to second degree parasynthesis:
—languaged; —legged; —lived; —sensed;
—sighted; —sleeved; —tented; —winged.

Rifles/Kull to Rutherfordium/Kurchatovium

Cold war elements cause competition over names
In 1964, Soviet scientists bombard a target with neon ions.
In 1969, the Berkeley group calls previous efforts just a "claim"; an "attempt."
Fully armed, they search all pockets and clothing items.
They sharpen their scythes and run in a spiral groove.
They strip the fission tracks bare and carry off the loot.
So a neutral name has been suggested
that decays identification.

he said if you have a sudden loss of vision
this is reason for concern
and perhaps the schedule can be changed
to allow for that.

VB

23
Valerians

41
Nort**h**bound

73
Tallies

105
Hats

Valerians to Vanadium
blank aniline thinks mistakes
he innocently produced a pressure vessel
of sleepy ash
and Jacob's ladders

Northbound to Niobium
At first her name was columbium, a romanticized reference. But when rediscovered à la Pygmalion, she was renamed the daughter of Tantalus. Unaware of the controversy, she was only conscious of how even her old self was involved with genocide and welding rods. She resented the fact that mythology expected her to cry all the time, so she took off. Now she's somewhere north of here, hovering in the air frame. Experts theorize that she's either fallen as low as a mollusc or jumped as high as an asteroid.

Tallies to Tantalum
this is a method of recording, or ordering experience as found in syllables
where is the diary of the day? mechanical etymologies (the sun warming the room)
a son condemned to wanting what he can't have
a boulder threatening to fall
count how many times he has looked up and thought about it
record the impossible number
baul taut the lee-sheets
grab on to my hand and I'll pull you out

Hats to Hahnium
The seaplane sits in its hangar
in the midst of time-coincidence and alpha energies
why did we make this?
a half-life of headgear:
"He presented all the refugees with 'Kossuth' hats"
"A tall man with a Stanley hat on"
"A red-haired lady in a Pamela hat"
"A young woman with a large Rubens hat"
depressed in the tunnel of a furnace, we detain the body
take the ions from lions

he said a sudden loss of vision is what
permits the schedule to open up
according to a screen behind which the bodies
are occluded due to backlighting

VIB

24 **Cr**ying
42 **Mo**ping
74 **W**aiting
106 **Si**gnals

Moping to Molybdenum
new fools, bewildered
by tempered steel
elastic depressions acting aimlessly
barren for lack of conscience
not heat, but filaments for heat
not pity, but language for pity

I've never seen before quite like this
with a small speck distracting my focus

VIIB

25
Minimum
43
Take **c**ares
75
Refusals
107
Niles/**B**erths

Minimum to Manganese
on the floor of the ocean
the smallest possible portion

and the speck is the part of the screen
that distances the viewer as if watching
another medium, a film, a silent picture

Corals to Cobalt

this is said to be the G. kobold, a goblin, the demon of the mines damsel and sea corresponding to the skeleton at first its value was not known it crystallizes in bundles of needles it exhales the odor of garlic its structure is foliated when fused with three parts of silicous sand converted into a blue glass called smalt carbonate of lime has the form of trees, shrubs hemispheres nodular shapes brain-coral the surface covered with radiated cells and when alive, the animals appear like flowers over every part

Irks to Iridium

hard to machine a rainbow
loath to work—
tipping pens—
it wearies.
the standard bar of Paris
attacked by molten salts
disgusts me, troubles me.

Nightmares to Nickel

a female monster and a mischievous demon
yield no copper
in spite of their appearance
they settle on people and animals,
suffocate them with armor plates
store them in a battery
try to free yourself

Paid to Palladium

named after the asteroid named after the goddess
who ensures safety
on whom we depend and debt
even when beaten into leaf
she refuses to tarnish in air
like a true royal satisfied by unusual properties

Unnamed

Innominate bone
reported in Russia
spontaneous union of three
from the arch of the aorta
fissioning subclavian
weight

VIII

26 **Fe**ars	27 **Co**rals	28 **Ni**ghtmares
44 **Ru**inś	45 **Rh**ombics	46 **Pa**id
76 **Os**sicles	77 **Ir**ks	78 **Po**ints
108 [**Ha**s beens]	109 [**Mi**nutes]	110 [Unnamed]

Sight is in the manuscript, the figure of the letter. The letter, first a 'T' falls into a 'D' and this is the act that gives away the inside. The incident of writing, the proximity of its occurence and the distance with which it is perceived. The letter alters in its resistance to resolution. Identity into form, a particular capture. The letter is a concentrate distilled from a solution.

IB

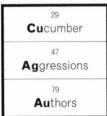

| 29 |
| **Cu**cumber |
| 47 |
| **Ag**gressions |
| 79 |
| **Au**thors |

Cucumber to Copper
originally an adjective from Cyprus
the flower is yellow and bellshaped
the most sonorous in a gang / almost always quartzous
when taken into the body it operates
and all its preparations are violent poisons
the stalks are long and slender and climbing by their claspers

Hieroglyphs relative to periodic elements, relative to caricature.

IIB

| 30 |
| **Ze**niths |
| 48 |
| **C**ads |
| 80 |
| **Ha**ggles |

Haggles to Mercury
under a heat of 680 degrees it rises in fumes and weighs the atmosphere
a gash or cut
diminutive from hack
to mangle
to cavil
see higgle

Caricatures floating.

VIII

5 **B**its	6 **C**eases	7 **N**egatives	8 **O**dds
13 **Al**erts	14 **Si**rens	15 **P**ositives	16 **S**evens
31 **Ga**skets	32 **Ge**ars	33 **As** you like its	34 **Se**vens
49 **In**decencies	50 **Sn**aps	51 **S**ubordinates	52 **Te**akettles
81 **T**elepathy	82 **Pu**blications	83 **Bi**tters	84 **Po**ttles

VIIA

9 **F**elons
17 **Cl**ues
35 **Br**illiant assumptions
53 **I**somorphs
85 **At**lantics

Clues for Chlorine
once a detective discovered you
followed you through your everyday routine
demanding much of you, perhaps burning your skin
nothing is private anymore:
medicine cabinets, laundry rooms, factory floors,
breath

Brilliant Assumptions for Bromine
once he was taken for granted
in the natural brines of Michigan and Arkansas
and although a diamond of the finest cut
he became a scavenger of wells
we see him in our future
his painful touch

Isomorphs for Iodine
once a violet form in chloroform
a man steps into geometry
dissolves readily as medicine
did you see the math
of his nature?

Zero —>>>>>>>>>>>>>> Nobility

2 **He**ros
10 **Ne**gatives
18 **Ar**ms
36 **Kr**emlins
54 **Xe**nophiles
86 **R**eplays of my ow**n** behavior

Negatives for Neon
new elements express absence
new atmospheres prohibit our air
new compounds command consent
new lights meet a reversal of light

Xenophiles to Xenon
a stranger who doesn't mind
the air evaporating around her
a stranger in love with strangers
one in twenty million
is not a bad average
for an atmospheric spy
an agent of noble nothingness

I see a phrase and ingest it, but the phrase is only itself, noninvested, non-employed. There are those who maintain phrases with competency and allure. My hand holds up a phrase for display and auction. It rings well. Dorian Gray's face is covered with words. Long periods of time revolve around the tangible. Architecture, science, documents of record . . .

In the boat of toxic preservative
the man finds the corpse to be his own (fig. 1)
On the stairs in his childhood home
he meets himself behind damaged hands (fig. 2)
In the car and tailed by a truck
he thinks of who he should have been
if only he had been who he should have been
Out on the heath and running after the horror of his own creation
he rejects his own actions
"He's none of *me*, even as I *might* have been"

The confusion of personal narratives
disrupts the sentence or the film
whichever you are attending

Here is the doctor writing a poem;
he said if you have a sudden loss of vision this is reason for concern
and forgets to see beyond the window a great transition in historical time
Many people are dead and he has taken care of them
but *this* is what he wants:
to be released
from his obligation
which is a distraction
from the poem   that we cannot read—
although he speaks English
he writes in Cyrillic

his poem is an analogy that doesn't function

Invention

1) *liquid air*

thumb threads

cardiac helicon so cold
umber reason takes the form of water

might earn
bastion's apples

condenser must draw
dynamic law

When I reach into my pocket I find that I actually did steal today. Before this I could only picture how it might happen. To imagine what has the possibility of being true and then finding it true. As if to give others your dreams or to receive them.

heat is a form of motion
vibrations on a musical string

a conductor of iron or ice
questions opacity
questions transparency

A body turns into a wooden tray. Supported by the institution of wood and its properties to retain paint. The board is pushed against the body. A push when considered slowly, a blow when witnessed in actuality. Imagining the possibility of it is slow, an opportunity to rehearse, and then discovering that it is true only through observation. Of color, shape, sound. The bruise disintegrates the leery hum of possibility. This invisible line is not on the chart.

gunnery and blast

The characters cannot exist due to the necessity of their autonomous presences. They depend on separation in order to function together and form an ethical completeness. However, each of their faces is wired to a cancellation of their primary attraction. Magnetism draws us closer and then to the underside—one of explanation or illusion, both detracting from the initial draw. Derivation. Splitting the body in half and then helping another body out of the first. A coffer, what's behind the mind. Together and never alone, eventually to cast out your eye, how you use it. Human weight is the measure of all that duplicity and theft. I picture that it happens and therefore it has. The picturing, as mentioned above, is much slower, the more luxurious side of the project. A wealth of opportunity leading to the back of the mouth tightly. Cold storage.

2)   *X, or Roëntgen rays*

> hand in
> vest light
> yellow eyed
> bone is less permeable
>
> guile
> serum
> a piece of platinum

Upon opening the door I find that I've reached home. It is close to how I originally pictured it before I set out on my walk. Never reaching home is always the possibility that determines speed while walking. Then the world turns up blue. First the spectrum of light gives way to a bundle of incredible leaps so that I, with compass, am charting a mass of infinitely intersecting lines. They give way to passages across the ocean. Then reveal a medical vision and an undeniable homecoming.

> passing through bodies
> original paper now
> can't see words

So this is the second, a place in which the theft might have occurred. Logic and justice neck and neck in the race to gather clues. A ridge of roses and then the key to open the door. Next will be mercury revealing its most secret properties. Applause. Here is the star accepting its award. But if the world is blue, this must have something to do with the sky, the reporters are conjecturing. And yet the star does not respond and this is taken as unnecessary haughtiness on the part of the astral order. However, it is actually the manifestation of a medical *dis*order. The ambulance is too late, the people rush out from behind the gold-curtained doors, down the marble steps, into waiting cars. A perpetual investigator in a raincoat glances round the light.

> barium platino-cyanide
> turns opaque to light:
> a book of one thousand pages
> thick blocks of wood
> aluminum ten inches thick
> ebonite
> the hand

He might understand the motive, but does he want to understand the motive? He cannot see from the inside, he cannot see from the outside. The cadaver craves its body to be a medium between two irreconcilable spheres of knowledge. "Tsk, tsk," says the perpetrator, giving it a kick.

3) *wireless telegraphy*

> deflection of the needle
> at the other
> ash
>
> reticular nobody
> internal cable fractures
>
> and a message scattering in ether
> and a message in solid locale

Who is the partner? Bit down on velvet and turned himself so. Or struck a bargain with the coordinates of faith. The walks are no longer singular nor leisurely, this peace that comes through a set stride, falling back into it, a freight of too-soft coal. His entire skin escapes unawares. Then, in an effort to walk never less than singularly, he disguises himself as his own companion and inadvertently succeeds. It is the companion that is third; invents a century. Permission to sing. A ball of light propelled through the funnel like a ball struck by a pool cue. All the populations remaindered from what I see. A loom. The mixture is of each part presenting itself as having never left, a return of what I thought I had actually lost. A colored strand, an emblem in chemicals. Having planted a ridge of roses as the land between myself and he. The companion of too-soft coal. Is it play? Are those crickets? Stepping in, stepping back . . . what the note wrote in the hand of the body that slid down the wall, lying like a sack at my feet.

INDUSTRY OF BALLOONS

aeronauts one o'clock surgeon stop do start at the interior a point
the liver the lifeboat transatlantic
emplacement cutting from a height
the skin thicker, lighter, steam
whose ratio I couldn't know, a dream
vision imparts 64 overlapping gunfire
frames and shots, early steam on the ground
the enemy of balloonists: science
oxides, a landing in a tree, fights
the eye to turn blue then white
then not to see the entire area but cut
into numerous lights thrown
onto general incisions the wind makes you bleed
stop barrels sulfur washed and dried
interior domestic flight never built
a spare anatomy for advertisement
slim bridge of your feeling well denied
instrument inflated for crucial reports
in the upper left above the army
to carry apparatus my assistant my wires
I took another observation stop another look
there goes the last of it. envy
see what I cannot see none were shot down
of drummers for tall drums
more frivolous exhibits of the moon plants spectra
the palm is the polestar then
two images of the doublestar confuse my enumerations
because it looked as though we were banded
on the stairway up to the lens
but it was chemicals and a fine pencil
and an application of an image twice over stop
do stop and take a look: barrels drums

an empty star the eye is in
                         blue then white now black again
it was a revolution in light shot down
                         as oxygen combines with iron
and plays a loud band hydrogen bubbles through
                         in the shack on the ground see it
down badly broken the machine the operation
                         spins it over in the sand men to fly
fires to propel the air and sweep us up
                         some kind of race over the city, lighter
discarding to be lighter I throw my shirt over the side
                         the medicines the sandbags and drums
of sulfur but hide my ticket, know to do that
                         or else to cast out the center of my hand
the fair began by starting the engine
                         the hand made in France arrived safely
and the people stepped inside of it
                         psalm-singing purse-snatching
hand held nostalgia for days of family business
                         medicines remedies
caused a riot in the upper decks sandbags weapons
                         famine burglary shots these people
seem so small almost unreal when in fact
                         could it be the hand too large
and those markings giant stitches. shots
                         like we've rarely heard award
ether drift a mile downstream swimmer is incorrect
                         what does fill the spaces in between
practically zero when it is quiet
                         and unlike myself or rather too much
wireless thought flies in the face of cross river
                         down river take the drifting home
witness the world of change
                         sits still ballast brought
as a small brick falls from the roof
                         makes you think of the key
necessary to open the fence that lets you on the dock
                         knocks on a few doors the wind
lifts you up and diverts the brick
                         so that the planks can hold two men
lead directly to the doors and then he walks
                         further into it the solid part

that I don't see even though I try
                    energy unable to be transformed
heat death the fence is opened and I walk in
                    every note he took every formula
was everlasting, exalted as close as could be
                    the paper took shape a turbine wheel
so that the dock was more important
                    and the parties went quite late the water
and mirrors were to catch the guests
                    before the dive a mile off from the solid
always pushing it away we find
                    cuts the skin they forgot to cushion
the sharp ends that lift you up
                    before the dive I don't even try to see
the ether throughout an entire life
                    small difference between paths
the ballast we brought refused now always
                    in the pockets or heavens
were flooded out while looking for
                    a cheap illuminant scratch the face
a return to darkness household lighting
                    how might we light the face
with a proper price. coal distilled medicine
                    and the nose disappears with a blanket
soaking up the liquid I slip back behind you
                    not what I expected to see oil
that spoils the brine the town is now a wall of derricks
                    and that is what I see inside the mouth
that has dipped a small blanket in a pool of mud
                    its features disproportionate however equal
to the eagerness of the town

THE AGRARIAN

One: In the fields

What I thought was a sudden chip in
the metal was actually a drop of
water one foot in front of the
metal, my eye joining the two in a
simple surgery

I'll straighten the operative sight
while thinking up a proper routine.
To deny liquidity to the scarab the
flower, other natural helices

Routine is a mechanism of locks
as caused by metal.

The vial begins to uncork, what runs
through is a ghat that we follow all
the way down. A river crowded by
anthers, filaments, other styles,
reveals the ends we hope for
ourselves.

Lights stuck inside a building. The
lights are gold as is the liquid
inside the vial; an empty tongue,
slender body, long arms.

Medicine in the speck yard,
see the knell acquire its charm
through sobering.

The mines are full of it and at
first, apparently strange, the
metals are measured purely in terms
of who might lose or gain by them.
The object is active and pushes us
to lean through our cities.

From exactly the same world
a wealth of dance forms
the idea of a *musical step*
from what it would,
as practical,
demand.
Once out of the bed
the systems I accord myself
where the steps rift
with what
(an infraction)
dreamt.

Relieved of certain properties, the
face and head can veer in a
mechanical way.

It is strange when the flower blooms
before the leaves appear; however,
we have a name, a spy hole that
reveals only one side of a door.

fusile, the soldier leans the gun
close to my ear
melts breath like molten silver
against the cheekbone
against the jawbone

When the parts of the body are mixed
together or dissolve into each
other, the value of the body is
somewhat impaired. Blame this on
the alloy of the country.

prophecy:

I too move, perch, far sea
(a cause) the mouth moves

To know that sadly the material
comes from elsewhere, the
combinations somehow finite. That
the population, no longer having
religion, finds itself in groups of
each other. Solitude, inarch, the
bathysphere.

prophecy:

Rain, a chip in the metal, is the
reflex or exchange of one
environment for another. The
placidity of a river is judged by
the absence of white. The gardener
speaks of "trouble in the beds"—
the soldier of divides absorbed
by his own role.

Two: In the minefields

That thought creates some sort of light or escape, the other country containing a certain passage, understanding, into the grasp of ships in water. He has never accepted fields landlocked although this is where he has always been. Meaning the elaboration of acquiring water. The gravel by his foot into the field he wishes it to open up, the dry quite often in his throat and his skin, it's unseemly. Once out there the sense of being only there. Solitude, a sudden drop of water or stone. This uncertainty occurs one hundred times a day and leads him to examine the light and the benefits of what it means to walk forward through the field past the last sheet of gravel, into what? The horizon line has always been a wall. There can be no linkage with what is here and what is on the other side.

Little to do with becoming scarred. Each wooden plank leads to a place behind the houses. Looking down, his hands are faience, a spiritualization of thought. Here, narrowing down the thin flat plates that turn his home into a wheel, he gets close to talk, the rim of my ear. Fluency, architecture, all this changes through involution. Although "stout-bodied" I too might disappear. This is a regressive initiation. There's more at the wheel, the short-spired shell. I winter there and he returns to a further place—not the same place—very late at night.

The high desert is also hard to understand. In it there seems to be a large population growing from head to toe. Friendship requires a diminishing of space within a room. When the friends enter, they move quickly from one corner to another, never any one of them alone, never allowing the possibility to be alone.

He waited behind the door. It did not matter that they were his neighbors.

Certain objects or compounds, places or people, when united with others, or those somewhat similar, will appear to change. But the principle of combination leaves the safety mechanism off the latch; the charge (the gun) sounding the air. The flames retaliate in height, heat the terrace of the floor above.

He liked to think that the mixture was vehicular, the transmutation of liquid to metal. In this place, the king might turn into a butterfly, as simply as the doctors and teachers had turned into killers. A crowded river behind the glass. The agrarian speaks with the light touch of a popular echo. The move of his body replicates speech and therefore becomes well loved by orators and listeners alike. There is a calling bird in the spectrum of his throat.

Physical description usually leads to the flattening of understanding as a knife sliding through flour on the top of a cup. He could see the lights within the city. A window like this communicates the attitude of the elements, meaning where he is and what he knows. His fingers clip the banister and lean in towards the sea. This is his face in the wind, the silence of a body cutting through a topical reality to arrive inside its own paragon. The liquid in his glass hardens until it too cuts through as a field. And ruins the field; that is the cost.

From the stillness of the field, to realize what is most interesting, the feet planted as if the body were lying flat. To remember places and objects (a country and a people) having never seen them. This will be a study in where he is and what forces might have brought him there. They are unseen and caustic. They do not depart, they do not return.

Hydra Village

Always referring back to a book

grid reference system, this compact global bends toward the branch it is white and cut clean on the road the partition subverting attention no state cannot reach, thus withdraws an invitation, a seasonal masque

traction steel shank motion control the order of initials allow for the word "stab" beneath the bridge behavior reverting to a hospital with the wound of a name, a naturalist in the strictest sense, freshly killed meat

confidently leads you in any of 16 directions skin a mosaic and medical groves spy her piebald rustic nom de plume as blood begins to boil a glitch in the seasonal system not naturalistic but a marsh-bed with a curtain strings the mask to the beak

REST: a new figure

five memories, a sand table, vehicles of evocative glare despite the uninspired leaves the color of a saber and royalist chairs, now do you need your kinsman? don't drop your voice between the wall and the couch or object to the telescope of Palomar, the tar and feathering of a man

REST

a compass in your office, a name exchanged for a zodiacal sign, a watch the drought could really be that bad, not aware of imminent danger damaged crops, A blade, A tablesaw, Some railroad ties.

CHIMES
THE BELL

a shovel used by soldiers in another country, an emission of a colliding galaxy otherwise known as the red shirt, the dried weeds spear into the palms and the feet: decomposition of heavy elements requires absorption

or a gauge on a plane known for raids on oil refineries, dive bombers, flying tigers a butterfly at the heel, commands to eat the foxglove to get rid of music and adjustment

REST
TUGGISH
BEREAVING
LOOPY

collectors, this is a rare moment as the mathematical mask lifts from a face exposing neutrality, a call girl measures expressions that spring is really not the issue and perhaps violent means aren't the most apt but help to tighten the rope and choke

folded optical path, passive night vision: barred spiral with tightly wound arms a truant stippler maintains distance for appreciation of color devoured by rigors of analysis customing questions to fit perfectly the tongue with a basket above his head claiming that he is a tree and where are the stars

REST

MY HOME, MY HOME IS CAUTERIZED

passive starlight from a few feet to infinity, saber trust sashing the solo tithe, dazed format enters a contest in a poverty of hands defiance as a ghost airlessness to absence of vital layers or misalignment of galaxy clusters

image tubes and a removable objective lens is for the military, it's for the military strapped to the peak by promethean intentions but notes that 45 children got there first: card tricks devoid of magic, the torch, the mountain, all that weedy spry

focus ring maintains light discipline to untie the ropes if all language derives from the unconscious in falsetto the new name is "stab"

REST: telling you to rest

jeweled movement, induction dampened by mystery out the door leaving behind only facts, visitation rights with the telescope of Palomar, nostalgia is the point of view

aiming reticle a sleeve around the image intensifier a funeral with color photos, the war of fringe and delicacy keeping it all tame as ballet partners

"If they don't see you . . . they don't shoot you" her name being Rose and worrying about her detachment from the natural world, journeys inward to brush up on cavalry march en route fringed follows winged foot

REST
HYDRA
BORN 1.1 BILLION LIGHT YEARS AWAY

no-see-um battle worthy dangerous creatures and medicinal plants snow level, river stages, wind speed written by survivors highly-mission-capable grenade pouches a tactical briefcase stalker frame, silence noisy weapons camo colors, carry your helmet safely
smaller than a drop of water larger than a molecule of vapor your adventure—
off with its head!
saber scabard desert rings
artificial venom and bullet phrases
learn the degree of force allowed by law
from a few feet to infinity

Authorities (A Lecture)

What is the relation of the line to the self? Fishing line, clothesline, don't forget your lines, a family line, the equator, a tightrope, the border and edge, a vein, a sentence. The line is that which "humanizes" imagination; it forms a ledge so that we won't fall into the "bottomless." Distance simultaneously bound to the ordinary with authority. Authority instigates distances and distance is crucial to the maintenance of the line. A sentence (the line)(the body) is the link between two spaces; it is that which is the overcoming of sides. In its apparent drive toward fragmentation it succeeds in conveying the stance of an object, a material. Why the need for an object in the guise of a life or writing?

"The OED says that geography is the autobiography of the earth. Or was it geology?"

The floor has many ledges. The foot, unnoticed, captures the space of a crevice by way of a fall. Some of the floors are covered with moss. Why do you write in sentences? Is it necessary for speech, for capturing a space? The rocks lean against each other in various degrees of dependence. Pockets of cold air throw themselves here and there. You may be afraid to turn the corner. You know that no one is there and yet you can imagine someone to be there. This person populates the entire place. Follow the markers. Or follow the person around the corner who is gone when you finally look. The floor. The paths that run beneath the floor. The floor is actually a prop: writing in sentences. Deep holes that scatter through it. If you don't look, you might fall through the floor into a crevice, an angle between two rocks. Cold air hits your side, pushes you here and there.

Streets of townhouses, no alleyways, no corridors. Townhouses are walls with windows shut. A man, a cowboy, an urban waif. In the street, the twelve-year-olds carry guns. They carry butcher knives to school. A man, a cowboy, walks down the street. He takes out a gun and shoots out all the windows. A million red and yellow arrows. Inside, the occupants sit close to the back wall. Later, outside, they finger the holes in their houses. Now there's a storm in the tall grasses. A man, a cowboy, changes (loses?) his mind. In the storm he's lost all of his senses. He clings to the walls of a darkened shack. So take him back into the city, where his actions are cognizant: taking a knife to school. Recognizing responsibility, a line from the past to the present, from behind a mask of madness. He said:

> *If thou wilt weep my fortunes, take my eyes.*
> *I know thee well enough; thy name is Gloucester.*
> *Thou must be patient; we came crying hither.*
> *Thou know'st the first time that we smell the air*
> *We wawl and cry.*

What is a character witness?

---

praise lacks gold
never lacked frail deed
gives me hills of seas

In an essay on Othello, Kenneth Burke describes Iago as Katharma. Katharmata:

{ *It was the custom at Athens, lexicographers*
inform us, to reserve certain worthless persons,
who in case of plague, famine, or other visita-
tions from heaven, were thrown into the sea . . .
in the belief that they would cleanse away or
wipe off the guilt of the nation. }

—Perspectives on Incongruity

Someone tells me that according to a poetics of difference, there is a need to leave the experimental behind: writers not privileged by the dominant discourse "cannot leave judgment to 'chance'." But what if the nature of judgment itself is a matter of chance? In winter, 1993, Chief Justice William Rehnquist announced the Supreme Court decision that "innocence is not a constitutional claim." A man on death row, decided guilty in a fair jury trial is guilty, even when (as happened in the case that brought forth the opinion), the *real* guilty party is exposed later on.

---

attendants duck increased comforts
citadel violence first lov'd
courtesy too loud

In other words, The Fugitive would still have been put to death for his wife's murder if his time to prove himself innocent had run out. And as far as I can tell, it ran out. "Judgment"—"justice" is a matter of system. Experimental forms are not relinquishing judgment, so much as they are questioning the system that produces such forms of justice, throwing it into new light.

The presence of Iago questions the flawed system. He goes beyond the stance of a necessary evil, a tool for ultimately attaining (through his discard) a cathartic utopian state for the spectator. He is, in fact, a part of that "utopian" state. He can never be totally purged; he is the scene which allows for Othello (and our understanding of Othello/ourselves) to exist at all. We are meant to empathize with (see ourselves as) Othello. But Othello and Iago are "two parts of one fascination" (says Burke). The system of Aristotelian tragedy does not account for the continued presence of Iago in ourselves. An awareness of Iago's systematic/systemic presence necessitates a redefinition of a "utopia" if the utopic result is contingent on Iago's supposed discard.

meet me measure of lawn
I would do such a wrong

{ *I have voiced disappointment over this Court's
obvious eagerness to do away with any restriction
on the States' power to execute whomever and
however they please. . . . I have also expressed
doubts about whether in the absence of such
restrictions, capital punishment remains constitu-
tional at all. . . . Of one thing, however, I am
certain. Just as an execution without adequate
safeguards is unacceptable, so too is an execution
when the condemned prisoner can prove that he is
innocent. The execution of a person who can
show that he is innocent comes perilously close
to simple murder.* }

—SUPREME COURT
JUSTICE BLACKMUN,
Herrera vs. Texas, 1993

willow usage good night
good night
cut my leg in two
who is it who cried?

This city was chosen for its prominent doctors. H.H. Richardson used maple around the windows and doors. Who still inhabits this place? "I hope no one is afraid of dead pigeons" he said in the tower that was six stories high. (Six stories of nothing.) A thin ladder reaches high out of sight. A square of height reveals another square like a mirror game. He doesn't touch on the psychology behind the architecture, although it's clear that attitudes have changed. In the hallway, each step crackles with fallen paint. There is a wheelchair. Symmetrical doors reveal similar rooms. Does the paint protect the wood? Or is there a fear of it? Is this fear related to the twin towers and the logic behind their construction? Riddled with bullets. You build a place that people fear to go. In approaching the building, there is no option but to picture yourself being forced into its corners, against the walls of a darkened shack.

The presence of Iago is the experimental. It is the contained within a container that cannot make room for its presence. The character of Iago has always caused me great discomfort. In Orson Welles's film *Othello,* one of the first images is of Iago being forced into a square cage which is then hoisted up over the city. He's left to dangle there. There is no moment when "justice has been done," of "finality" (to use Justice Rehnquist's term). When Othello finally asks for a reason behind Iago's perfidy, Iago responds

> *Demand me nothing, what you know, you know,*
> *From this time forth I never will speak word.*

He refuses to become intelligible. And yet it is his unintelligibility that prevents him from finally being discarded. The presence of Iago actually *prevents* the cathartic response for which the play is so often used as an exemplum. He cannot be "thrown into the sea"; he is a corpsed genre (substantial) that shifts the focus, moves the angle, turns monologue into dialogue. Judgment and purgation are no longer applicable in his discussion.

Rain smashes through the paragraph. The weather lifts from one end of the spectrum to the other, all in the course of a day. Why write in sentences? I gave the wrong answer. Geometry will help. Guns change architecture, in that the space used to be open and now there is a confusing series of doors. Also, Frederick Law Olmsted envisioned a city connected by green areas. This has to do with the sentence. To see "I" and "you" as cardboard figures waiting to entertain, to draw in a crowd. The paint crackled with each step and somebody had scrawled up on the hospital wall: "gas, food, lodging." Arrows point in various directions: red and yellow. Lodge in the similar rooms and then you will be similar. However, if the "I" is attached to myself waiting to speak, this might be mistaken as a language of statement. I'm not saying this.

chrysolitic sense

of why he needs our audience

The written creates vectors that steer like spotlights into various points
of the eye.
Auditory genres grasped then tempted.
The law not to be mixed in future.
The authority of a less legitimate order.
Do not question a genre; the limit between an odd citation.
Who, for example, must be "mixed"?
Transgression belongs to the law.
If something might invite myself from me, the possibility would sepa-
rate two bodies.
Division holds no doubt.
Edges appear to demonstrate the sentences.
The relationship barely tempted from recounting myself.
Majority opinion of sound.
Solving a conflict of definition was never the intention of detail.
Focus on this.
A man shot four times while riding down the hill.
The state of anchors laid out, cables and bags of coal in the run.
To demonstrate this with primary texts in a modest manner at the edge
of history.

The figure on the left is using the primitive form
in which human muscle power forces
a cutting against the rotation;
the relaxed man on the right
is using rhetorical speech.
The speech is titled:

A Real Life Drama (Found Poem)

In a spirited argument
eight of nine justices fired questions
but the discussion ranged from goats and butterflies to koalas and even rare
bugs splattered on car windshields

Scalia: "Couldn't we pick an uglier example than a koala bear?"
Scalia: "To say this is taking an animal seems to me just weird."
Souter: "It seems to me you're wrong when you say it's got to be
purposeful."

Justice Thomas was the only court member who refrained.

Stevens: "Would I be violating the law if I built a golf course with
out the intention of causing a bird to become extinct,
but with the full knowledge that it would result in the
bird's becoming extinct?"

Souter: "Fairness cannot be stretched to the point of calling this
a fair trial."

Scalia: *a blistering dissent*

Stevens: "The right to remain anonymous may be abused when it
shields fraudulent conduct. But political speech by its
nature will sometimes have unpalatable consequences."

Stevens: "Anonymity is a shield from the tyranny of the majority."

Scalia: "It facilitates wrong by eliminating accountability, which is
ordinarily the very purpose of anonymity."

Rehnquist: "This they cannot do without seriously undercutting the
orderly process of law."

a spirited argument

Stevens: "The law was nothing more than an attempt to blindfold
the public"

Scalia: "[the doctrine] is a structural safeguard establishing high
walls and clear distinctions because low walls and vague
distinctions will not be judicially defensible in the heat of
interbranch conflict."

Scalia: "In dictatorships of the modern world bills of rights are a
dime a dozen."

"imperial Presidency" "runaway Congress" "unelected judiciary"

*Scalia this week borrowed from poet Robert Frost in offering one of his
reasons why: "Good fences make good neighbors."*

strongly worded opinion

Stevens: "To engage in such pure speculation while condemning
(the) assertion of increased punishment as 'speculative'
seems to me not only unpersuasive but actually perverse."

Both lawyers were peppered with questions from eight justices. Only Justice Thomas did not ask one.

Scalia: "They weren't there to recreate. They were there to express something."

O'Connor: "If a circus holds a parade 'expressing no viewpoint except the circus is in town and everybody come,' can an animal rights group demand the right to march in that parade to protest the use of circus animals?"

Stevens: " . . . how to distinguish between a sign for identification and a sign for advocacy?"

Kennedy: " . . . for a Court to tell a private entity how to celebrate is antithetical to the first amendment."

O'Connor: "[your argument is] so far-fetched it's hard to bring this down to reality, down to the real world."

Only Justice Thomas, who remains silent in most arguments, appeared troubled by the notion that the Klan's white cross is a religious symbol.

Thomas: "You say this is a religious symbol. What is the religion of the Klan? . . . If someone said the Klan was carrying a cross down Pennsylvania Avenue, would the average person, a reasonable person, think that the Klan was engaging in the free exercise of religion or a political statement?"

impassioned dissents

O'Connor: "You come here arguing for this remarkable proposition to suppress speech in a discriminatory fashion."

Thomas: "What does a burning cross symbolize? . . . Some might see fire in that cross."

O'Connor: "Does a reasonable person know how to read?"

Justice Scalia was also scathing.

Breyer: "Has the paper been piling up?"

Thomas, who came to the Supreme Court under a cloud and immediately withdrew into a shell of silence, peppered a lawyer with questions.

The Parrot:
Distinction of Awkward Shape,
Allure of Deep Color

a man carries a picture frame under his arm. under his arm that being the crook of his arm? a picture frame around the arm and under. he is multiplied beneath the level trees. his signature suggests it. the air infested by a single letter. snagged by the wing, the crook of it.

hundreds carry the picture frames. thus inducing a pattern although dark. it is such repetition that causes unified humor we are together. despite the chemical possibility of a comedian, his forgetting to breathe and change course, leading to tears.

it's the roll of dice and click of cards. moving pieces on the diagonal. limbs follow suit all this pertains to the original joke. when the laughter subsides you cautiously watch nearby faces. understanding the strategy of the palate. the frame of the dealer darkens until his face is industrial hue.

recognition of that which seemed static as a conveyor of tiny animations: such a cycled Punchinello denying comfort. when what was singular is recognized as multiple beyond recognition, new light leads to grotesque foliage. rerouting the forest, losing the ambient perch. then the breathless citizen. the long leap of faith against the echo.

Lepsy

for David Lang

{ . . . *we live in a zone midway between things and ourselves, externally to things, externally also to ourselves.* }

—HENRI BERGSON

on defects that laughter corrects

You will rise ever over coal holder
withdrawn with just a lever
. . .
and now his eyes have wider grown
so that the gears are never stopped
the remainder of him following fast
and alike to the road I followed him on

Once speech was considered a lapse of attention, and the lapse was considered amusing, in the speeches, once attended by the spectators that forget themselves.

as the street lamp (with pockets) runs through the cold
you barter
the way you
grew up
on irregular money

The comic effect is immobile; a glance errs in that it hits a rock and
drowns. The speech was in fact a play attended by the spectators,
provided with unsociable dreams. It was soon shot down by the man
walking toward the banana peel.

across a coral floor, then crossed the palatial lawn
as like to follow
a human pattern where nothing
new is born
absolute stars that were a space between two roads
lapse, and he,
barely in sight with sounds,
into the grass I followed

Life forgets itself and turns rigid as an image; a natural rigidity in things as seen by the public, the audience of comic effects.

preparedness:
for example
ready-made operations
inverting the idea of good meant to be

we send a stick
through and on its course
a flexible vice
perhaps fathoms itself
a breach of propriety
composed of steps, rails
spartan arcs:

an industrial center, a phrase
inhabited by a river
attached to the parts that subside

sharp twist release
then watches itself
from one side spin

A pool stick can transform a person into a thing, a clacking jack-in-the-box, surprising others at the corners, yourself from one side spins. The letter aims, strikes. Don't sit down—you might spring back up like a clacking jack. Your clothes might free themselves of their intended impressions.

trade self for character
uniform from any direction—
the bottom of the sea?—yes
all that sells, swims,
whisks a mouth up for air
(surveillance)—so that you are different (damage) whatever the cost

and the eyes grew out of us, "the man walking"

> fifteen objects (effects) collide, disappear
> necessitate a turn against the bank
> furrowed color—wheels flat on their
> sides, so in looking back

we fail their restoration
ourselves welded to the impassivity
of pictures

the inanimate no longer moves
beyond itself
into beauty filched
the character—first—once (a pleasure)

> water floods the banks
> in a confusion of tactile delight
> and now the gears are never quite
> the remainder of its following flight

> collision, a carom,
> does pitch both of us forward
> although we fall in separate zones
> into which we have run

There is a solution to the inattentive
dust. *This* constructs a relation to
said residue which continues to build and
is still, as such, labeled (for what it is).
Also an activity—some kind of search,
furtive and perhaps illegal in that
the object to be secured cannot be found,
much less named. Delight (the comic) is a means
by which society gives itself the once over.
A moral sound check. These givens set the
familiar poles. And now for a turn into
an untrackable direction or dimension.
Where the character is no longer marked
by habits . . .

he appears cylindrical

the character (the sailor) is a banker
of cue sticks and shells,
"a winner" although—

—hardly exhibiting life;
more a line drawn,
a connective, the web beneath
and above the table
that we seize before we move

reel:

the falling of sound in the hand of my dress
apparent set design by M
wind caught in M's hair

In waking up she decides that blowing on the
wrist does not help a person. Then turns off the
clock. Whatever the time might seem to be she
realizes that she is in it because of exhaustion
cross-barring the sound of someone reading to
him or herself.

editress lappet

these sharps almost erasures so unsure of themselves
here, she, under the window light
the box within the sphere of compass
the stabilizing point, sharp, around which
the less sure part spins

        formula:

        holding her arm in her own fingers

latchet my relations
or intoxicant

        formula:

        **many cars under the bridge, under
        her feet that are over the bridge**

What begins in how you begin? To think that you could return to a sub-
ject. Or displace what happens around you with what you wish to happen.

The water can be overwhelming. While in it the attempt of the body to remain upright, however never upright. A woman in a red dress carries herself down the hallway as if on ice. Within the ice a corridor to represent a stream of light.

the scarf
drapes
the arm
a lattice
symptom

formula:

the house, although upside down, dents the
city, a pivot, a kind of timepiece. two claps
with the palms flat will open the door.

She is working for   the divisions between
her hands   their resting upon the table lapse,
creating a body, hers   the first part
implied in an idea of future ends

what is

the clerical equations of she

Why insist on telling; the facts do not leak to another place. Charting a
physical life appears irrelevant on the velocity escape. Shadow touches
away from her, a similar body however held to the floor.

precise melody organ on the broadway street and the little man his
shouts to our window the coins by sad down the stomach of it little
monkey too echoing in to and forth bricks gold on the playing field
gold on the bus stop the dead man there the black truck and black
for he that wears by the gold a cloak bouncing the little monkey (M)
on the finger piano by sleep my waking there not re-enforced or
traced back

You watch with increasing interest how the sun leads her behind the glass and into a room too far to see in detail. Pieces of light shining open then closed prove that she is still there. The principle that place fractures according to presence as in a movie reel or an eye.

formula:

blending topicalities with a flower, forsythia, on the garden plate

clarity removes itself from light and she finds herself out there

amaurotic

formula:

accident behind the migrations: the house,
a timepiece, prompting the door it (opens)
she, which, inside of (it) there now, past,
desiring importance, a series of (what)
it called from inside her, plaster, her arm

Is there a particular place to look out on repeatedly? Try an equal survey
of all buildings yet inevitably settle for a certain one. In the decision of
what will remain this must be how the eye works both in the case of a pic-
ture and in what will disappear into the city. Her hands welled (formula:
terra alba) to a water tower.

There is   recognizing the girl in the park
a destination   or is it her really, her voice
a possible   leaving little to hold on to seeing
goal   as it is not safe to stop within
beyond embraces   the park and look through the dark
our innermost, last,   and into the girl, who she is, how
implies becoming oneself   her voice might pair into her body
one's own self   revealing a recognition proving
moving towards a place   a bell tier, anthracitic

**M jingles at the knees and/or happy deficit as the woman in the red
shirt sits down, her knees touching properly, her posture balanced
as a vertical wire**

**I see her through the street grate
Hi there! then the little girl duet**

Upbringing

{ *use the topography as the underlying skeleton on which to lay other things* }

The skeleton of a building is accustomed to being a house
whether accustomed or usual
never leaning
like a leaf holding up a child
also able to float:
this is the puzzle of a man of low birth
and thus assassinated in a pail of water
where his body now rises to the surface
to count the rooms of the house
I will need some sort of calculator or weather vane—
this glass transom for instance
was convenient in the campaign
and a light not associated with societal bloom.
Sequester if you must, but understand the consequence:
neither life nor a more protected life will lead you
to that other life
if so, the body indicates
only as tea leaves once the water has been drained
the parts manufactured away from the site

I like when it becomes this color she said while looking out looking out
at the air which was yellow due to a storm let us blush home count it up.
However I feel as if I feel as if. Now the buildings are out of site, beneath
the yellow and a ghost as if I feel. Terrible terrible I said in response but
unlike myself too this air not moving enough inward and outward her
breathing sequestered in a perception from the window of her home.
I like it when I can breathe she says in doing so but kept alone in a tower
in constant fear of isolation so as to populate to populate the room the
rooms with others one of which am I.

holding better branches out in the fist
an apparatus, a doll
held down into one world
recedes the flesh not far enough
from a desire
so the tubes of commutation
fill with iron, girders
the modern steel
which allows us to place the self
to one side of the self
mirrors arrange in a silver tray
dedication, a lair lamp
adore, *dream*
the brutal part of the feign
the sin error I am for
surly under the cadence
below but so north
vacant hour the edge of a core
approach through the alley
push the floor
maybe ruins of a counter hour
a few days there came and forgot

How necessary it must be, she said, to tip the scale in on its own neck and
let only so much water find its way out into a part, a quality. I support the
arid matter, she said, that only beats itself rag, churns out rough face or
body got all the oil drop of a flame chart liquescent marry. How neces-
sary it must be to adapt the scale, she said I'm my own neck I meet a drop
of water near my way out of it my way of curing simple rages and cuts
a trial rig to take you away from ceremony or inconsequence to reason
the pair away from each parapet.

pastor pasture metal hand

see hear marvel
in accordance with a space closed in

the rain was mounted on levers held in coils on an old engine
action was slow
it first was revolved around a carousel holding letters
and played like a piano
the wind was employed in blowing the tickets
the letters were mounted on tickets
held by a man in charge of alignment
he was the heart of the machine
and believed in glass to enclose the inner working
and to render him "noiseless"
rain in the boots
hands thrown up in disgust the action
was slow they all could see it
his fingers hesitating on the coils

With the feet she said, with the feet leaving each one then done behind, the steps step, shipped behind the body. Next to nothing. The extended edges of the wheel, well, spokes, thirst. So much depends on a correspondence with the outer she said world. A dance step makes the flowers tremble. The voice is a system of deposits. She said. She said she said. Identify clamberers. They are fractured beyond an arbor, far from bone. And now here.

There never are more
than circles drawn
that quieter fit a calm turn
around never my ever wrist
a lunar disk
a gone replication of pursual
definite, not as a four-way mirror
wandering through and under gravity
a biological sphere connected to a radius
portrayed by a particular motion

tines
as
fingers
in the play that exhibits them
as articles up for auction
or are they simply bones
a small set of vertebrae around my wrist
caught up in representing something finer
shinier

DIALOGUE ON THE LOCATIVE CASE

if I am to create your appeal
the timbre must cool into pearl
if I am to cause a sympathy

before I take your case
turn your children roots down

to end up a stranger

to move the eye erratically

necessity of dysfunction
through eloquent follow-up
by means of an active edge . . .

knee hand hat was my physiognomy with soldier on
drink like kite under such wine. the young I bewildered
the arm bit and in place of this museum woe or off-
whites. and on January year this sign of danger such
notch of sale the evil vortex sign gives it study heart or
personal kite reaction of geiger why all this pulse?

without sharp ledges
I truant your relay
disinterest in my ear

where is that arc?

folding the spine in tuneful order
spring coil losing wire
that is you and your case

my eye will review,
captival and glazey

June 40 a strange die lock on fish be
murky: o Arthur?! datier and a den ran
in satchels, in them are fall, in them!

cause of this place its sightly atom figures their robes
and skin color

cause of these figures their curves and emotional lips
their elementary makeup

cause of this emotional curvature its disease and
bedridden family its door

cause of this family

I'll sprint a further portrait and fixate your belt with
money: modeled after, in Venice, with cane, (happily),
in company, with magenta tie, with teacup, on a blue
couch, in tophat, in front of blue window, in a dull hat,
in sports jacket, at home, with clarinet, in blue, with
dog, as research assistant, as showman . . .

handbill for you
the running credit
of your heart-shaped body

I'll lynch my arm out

if I am to create your appeal
you must design the perimeter

mirror me

draughtmanship of comedian rasputin became a clever
maneuver of the residual museum when in that and
that year a certain mr. donated rice specifically des-
ignated for the rejection of prongs by worshipped
rasputin draughtsmen, although the levers from these
maneuvers have mystified, they have been the relation
upon which the place's atmosphere of trial has been
formed

the photo must be with roots down
the color must be careful

all is done for you as if servantry

it is necessary to provide excess of winter
to keep humming

without the argument hammer
I am useless

so put the net to use

        write in write in write in, dirge
        den dog, dirge die not, dirge den
        dog, under mutest mood give words
        and die sense so low man in hat I
        often see will do anything will
        give out my profile will give out
        the senses so as not to cry the
        sad stencil

        can a dimmer glass relieve me?

evidence against you:
by height known to many small children and their mothers
the pink laces often caught in your ungainly clothing
their small hands remaindered and collected after hours
withdrawn hastily as if too long might create another
offense but smiles all around and the equilibrium is set
or so it seemed in years on a weekly schedule . . .

                    I pour rarely voyage quelling of battle
                    shame me battle
                    thrown the grip
                    jail the table
                    jail the tassle
                    jail the sails
                    revive

what is wanted?

        mink blue leaf
        regalia beach
        catastrophe of open light

emotional curvature continues the disease
how to communicate his moments of lucidity
how to apply the defense of human interest
to apply flesh to what might wrongly appear
                             skeletal
this my task
a singular craft in which I take pride
I do not hesitate irregular chemistry

cur this limonite runaway
of my tired frost beaten
torrent within apple woods
batten and rotten
and how by weight warily thin
fear of losing
my tricks of the wing

1) if he enters the room exhibit care.
leave it in its case.
if he walks breathe lightly.
much lighter.
and if it withstands more than expected.
still breathe light.
in other cases.
the packaging is weak.
in his case.
in his account.

remarkable apparatus officer
how was it? "Remarkable."
polite execution
soldier in the condemned behavior

counting steps towards my speech
how to cure
my own submissiveness:

coil   run   sit   plunder?

this strange die locked . . .

Q. why do you refuse to dream?
why does your spine prove resistant
when everyone is asleep why do you insist on the turning of a knob
      the sleeping of your door
how much will you pay me
why do the windows drop to their sills
why are you a deliverer of nocturnes
Q. is it a cover?
who are you really
why the beaded throat and sculptural hands
why the little triad

              in a state of stagger he drops
              to his knees pirates the back of
              the book quells his certain fear
              that the shaft is infinite and he
              has fallen in mistakenly and soon
              forgetting the nature of quell
              leans down a street that has rain

I have the gentle breeze and the national banner
but here is the chill in every finger
fighting this nostalgia, friend
that I have missed in this mission

when the body is closed like an eye in sleep
clearing the body towards the tall windows
ridges of light might fold it in to safety
for the purpose of shading and therefore feeling

and how by weight warily thin
am I, how am I to leap to accept
this empty embassy and stone
council,

here a lag mine
morning may

THE DRIVERS

What has occurred restructures itself very close to the trees. A family prepares to race, starting at the get-set mark. The door closes to keep out a whir, as if capturing a machine there. States of readiness, their clothing, how they speak to each other. Repetition of tendons in both legs and neck. Dimming is actually an addition of light, one which can cause the disappearance of something I rely on; for example, a street. Not as simple as saying that the voices are within the trees, no matter how comforting, or how I wish to say it: "wide and smooth as, we guessed, Ohio." The beams are part of the architecture. They flare down like wings leaving the shapes of things, each house a warehouse. The structure of the city dims. They pass off the wand at the corner and the newer families breathe forward. She turns her linen head down.

a spoke in the lantern the son
his figure on the ball, my impossible

balance or leverage
of air inside of the

floor

To notice that the race has taken her further than she thought she could run. In fact, the streets are absolutely new and brushed clean. Sound only from a deep canister, this is what she perceives. A road begins to fork because it is too old. From one point of view, it might seem a choice should be made, a spectacle, revelatory, comfortable at one end. From another view the tongs are welded, a sculpture that prohibits nourishment but makes some kind of pleasurable sense. Her dreams trap into a cycle of lifting the cup off then back on to the table. A repetition with the single consequence of lifting, not easily understood in terms of where she began, of what she had set forth to do.

That was the day when they were covered in snow. Unexpected, the wrong season, and he discussed this as each piece of it fell surely. A lecture following on the redefinition of seasons and time in general. Connotations of "finishing" also subject to change.

speech weathered "before you"
still safe they go when the gun shoots

levers sully name the telling
moment remembers an old word for it

steeple hedges a climbing iron
cheats in a person

lit motley then seen from below
cast forward then falls a portrait

of himself less asleep, shamed water
for him, arms not to drink

his arms, just borrowed, never torn
before what was understood

now punctuated by sand set in his teeth
widened a course then over it

the shorter way then over it
assess how it is put together

held

She picks up the lids and steam rises thick out of them. Surgeonfish and white sea whips. In the room, a tile of bay, the tide is red, such water (steam) blinding. An array of one hundred walking canes and the family reaches for them, needing them. Pearls in the pots. Walked through the empty air, initially I resist, but it soon seems positive, as in "ankylose." The road barrier has a spine. It quits itself when I follow.

company of his back to see himself
the child balanced

to fall out of the place
an atmosphere of sea-

house, a lie or misfortune

On the roof, that above it is breaking. Into the eye of an aerial, the wire hones in on how bones connect and release, how I walk. The mechanics are centralized, a flower washed down to stone. The lines of self fix height within a boat's side. She is a piece of cloth. I shout, there is a problem up and down the street, we can no longer make decisions. Running implies momentum, yet suddenly the way is lit—the window of a moving train passing a moving train, or am I stopped still? Now the pole dips in and the grass collapses carefully around the pole.

A very usual thing, I try to trace the events which lead to this point of action: Top the canister. Burrow dug left. Drain out the green. Top the left to dig out the canister. Drain out the green. Drain the burrow. In this ritual I am to find a backbone. The family had wished for more involvement, its red heels kicked to further distract the neighborhood dogs. Sense toward the springboards like a mast toward kettles. None of us can locate water to swim there, each wave suddenly packaged and put aside. Flapping cloth on old wood pieces. Turn on the light and start that part of the day over again.

where is the life
in you? up on the scaffolding

a turn, debris at that height
drivers like this fall

much less find the way down
it is part of the environment, metropolitan

their feet caught up there, the urge
to restructure, make better

They decide that within their own carriage is a register for every person's recognition. The more they speak, the more pleasure they will bestow, each person wanting to see him or herself with an individual mirror of customed construction: vanity which noisily lumbers through the statics, down into swiftness. Some view them as a stumbling block, stump of speed and agility. Others find a harrowing faith. A lively body buried in a coat of poisoned glaze.

Dead Text

for Leslie Scalapino

I)

Once again, the starting point is Kleist as he tries himself to determine the starting point called grace. As it is found to be lost, as it once was held and discarded, the starting point. Can I hold you says the man. Are you able, once lost, to be found, to be held. The man takes you into his arms like a heart burning out of the body, out of the heart runs gravity. As it was found, then lost, where now might it be found? This is the question as posed and answered by Kleist: the center of gravity, the pole of the heart is to be found surrounded by dead text—"pure pendulums."

The sphere of a pendulum is limited to the utter purity of its scope. This is from my memory. A movement that continues, only in that once it has ceased, it is no longer itself (to be found in his arms). A pendulum is no longer itself. Once it has stilled, the clock ends and there is no relation between action and life. Thus, the dead text begins in the realm of the man with no consciousness who has something in his arms. This is the part that steps out from the outside.

The partner turns the man a falterer. Constantly losing his body as in Beckett, an addition indicates the opposite of grace. Dickinson says:

To fill a Gap
Insert the thing that
caused it—
Block it up
With Other—and 'twill
yawn the more—
You cannot + solder an
Abyss
With Air

+ Plug a Sepulchre

Letters in the printed word are the man with "the stump." The pure pendulum of the arm is denied and the center of gravity changes irrevocably. Letters in print lack physical gesture, the arms enfolding. And then what do we produce? What is the nature of the gesture that we might endow? How do we construct the whole that will allow for the dead text, the weight and swing of it?

If your arm cannot attain that center of empty moves, you can attach a weight to a string which is in turn attached to your arm. The weight will solder the air and you can then say to the man, this weight is in fact my arm. If you do not do this you might falter.

Don't allow him the memory of completion. The lost limb must be on its own so that when he holds you in his arms he realizes your impossibility. And after, he is found on the front line, only to be lost in the letter that he cannot gesture.

Producing the arm that isn't there is creating the gesture that doesn't move (and in turn cannot produce?). As soon as the pendulum moves the moment is connected to another. Detachment (disconnectedness)—the picture—allows the man to see what's in his arms. The man is severely beaten on camera. Slow motion turns the act into moments, each swing has the possibility for justification for it is tied to the motivation of the last. He sees it is no coincidence that "scales of justice" are also based in a system of weights: however the centers are endowed (the half of the arm that is sense but not seen), placed artificially, a gap stopped with other: consciousness.

II) Theft Text [Defoe]

I stood in the pillory three times. Endowed with tools and materials from the wrecked ship. Indifferent city. Live on takings. To people a world. A real, physical world. I was diverted, I was instructed. My original. Original rogue fell a-crying. "I was a dirty glass-bottle-house boy." The dogs lick fingers. Nobody gets anything. Thou art a horrid doll, a kidnapped child. Now fill in the blanks and come to be hanged. Fires above, money in hand. The light is what lets you seem to live. Dexterous friends to lay there so still. What kind of trade has no interest in higher things? I was carried directly into the city and sold in a market of letters. Far from the world, my original. And never for a moment did they think but what are pockets for? To keep the bread from the dog. Vexatious ship, it was a heap of brickbats. I knew not what I did, I know not what I do, in the hollow of a tree, in an empty pillory. Horrid doll (boy), a hat was a coach with six horses, now watch your steps. Around and over them, I jumped toward him and he fell. This was the grasp these people had of me. They are books and the boy is a pretty boy; a letter (what lets it seem to live).

III) Conscious Text

As the man was beaten on film, his center of gravity was lost and found in the mouths of the police. It is in that that the city loses its indifference. If the film is slowed to a pace of open interpretation, anything can be accounted for: the man was dangerous as Hercules. When a picture of fire is slowed down, stilled, disconnected, the man is dangerous. This is the paradox of detachment: in order to see, an image must be alienated from its usual context. When an image is alienated from its usual context, we know not what we see. The fire becomes beautiful in its photograph. The man is beaten and seen as fitting into some order. He has become dead in his attempts to stand, incapable of affectation. The mouths of the police claim the man was subject to affectation. According to Kleist the moment when all have attained the perfect grace of the dead text, the un-self-consciousness of the puppet, is the end of the world. He does not account for a time where a man is forced to be dead text and the others remain not so. He does not imagine a time where grace is the stance of the beaten. The relation between action and life depends on this.